TRUSTING
the GOLD

ALSO BY TARA BRACH

*Radical Acceptance: Embracing Your Life
with the Heart of a Buddha*

*True Refuge: Finding Peace and Freedom
in Your Own Awakened Heart*

*Radical Compassion: Learning to Love Yourself
and Your World with the Practice of RAIN*

TRUSTING
the GOLD

UNCOVERING YOUR NATURAL GOODNESS

TARA BRACH

Illustrations by Vicky Alvarez

sounds true
BOULDER, COLORADO

Sounds True
Boulder, CO 80306

Published 2021

Cover & Interior Illustrations © 2021 Vicky Alvarez
Cover and Book Design by Lisa Kerans

Printed in South Korea

Library of Congress Cataloging-in-Publication Data

Names: Brach, Tara, author.
Title: Trusting the gold : uncovering your natural goodness / Tara Brach.
Description: Boulder, CO : Sounds True, [2021]
Identifiers: LCCN 2020025072 (print) | LCCN 2020025073 (ebook) | ISBN
    9781683647133 (hardback) | ISBN 9781683647140 (ebook)
Subjects: LCSH: Self-actualization (Psychology) | Self-acceptance. |
    Compassion. | Awareness.
Classification: LCC BF637.S4 B6685 2021 (print) | LCC BF637.S4 (ebook) |
    DDC 158.1--dc23
LC record available at https://lccn.loc.gov/2020025072
LC ebook record available at https://lccn.loc.gov/2020025073

10 9 8 7 6 5 4 3

CONTENTS

LOVE

FREEDOM

AN OPENING INVITATION

For decades a prayer has circulated in the background of my daily life: May I trust my own goodness. May I see the goodness in others. This longing emerged from a deep place of suffering I went through as a young adult. During that dark time, I felt anxious and depressed, separate from the world around me. I was continually judging myself as falling short, not good enough, doubting my basic worth. That of course kept me from feeling close and connected to others and to the world. It blocked me from feeling creative, stopped me from being fully alive.

It feels like grace that this "trance of unworthiness" led me onto a spiritual path that showed me how to hold myself with compassion. This allowed me to see through the layers of judgment and doubt and to discover beneath them clarity, openness, presence, and love. Increasingly over the years, my trust in this loving awareness as the essence of who we all are has become a guiding light. No matter how wrong or lacking we may feel, how caught in separation, or how trapped by the messages, violations, and inequities of the society we live in, this basic goodness remains the essence of our Being.

A beautiful story holds within it this truth. During the mid-1950s in Bangkok, Thailand, a huge clay statue of the Buddha began to crack due to heat and drought. When some monks arrived to investigate, they shined a flashlight into the largest of the cracks. What they saw surprised everyone. Deep under the gray clay was the gleam of gold.

No one had known that inside this popular but ordinary-looking statue was a solid-gold Buddha. As it turns out, the statue had been covered with plaster and clay six hundred years earlier to protect it from invading armies. Although all the monks who lived in the monastery at that time had been killed in the attack, the golden Buddha, its beauty and value covered over, had survived untouched.

Just as the monks disguised the beauty of the golden Buddha in order to protect it during dangerous times, we cover our own innate purity and goodness as we encounter a challenging world. As children many of us were criticized, ignored, misunderstood, or abused, leading us to doubt that gold within us. As we grow up, we increasingly internalize the judgments and values of our society, further losing touch with our innocence, our creativity, and our tender hearts. We cover over the gold as we seek the approval of others, looking to them to measure our worth—to determine whether we are good enough, smart enough, successful enough. And if we are part of a nondominant group in our culture, we take on additional layers of protection to help us face the violence of social injustice and oppression.

Adding layer after layer to protect ourselves, we become identified with our coverings, believing ourselves to be separate, threatened, and deficient. Yet even when we cannot see the gold, the light and love of our true nature cannot be dimmed, tarnished, or erased. It calls to us daily through our longing for connection, our urge to understand reality, our delight in beauty, our natural desire to help others. Our deepest intuition is that there is something beyond our habitual story of a separate and isolated self: something vast, mysterious, and sacred.

What helps us uncover that gold? How can we learn to trust the pure awareness and love, the basic goodness that is our very essence? How can our lives be an active expression of our natural wisdom and kindness? And how can we respond with a wise heart to the human ignorance, greed, and hatred that perpetuates violence toward each other, racial and other caste systems, cruelty toward non-human animals, and destruction of our living Earth? These questions have shaped my spiritual path, and in *Trusting the Gold* I share my own challenges and discoveries in stories that I hope you'll find meaningful on your path as well.

The three sections of *Trusting the Gold*—Truth, Love, and Freedom—explore the basic teachings of the Buddha that awaken us to who we are. We begin with learning to recognize the Truth of our experience by opening to life, just as it is. Then we discover how to awaken our inherent capacity to meet this ever-changing life with Love. This unfolding of presence and love reveals the Freedom of our true nature. You might find it beneficial to follow the sequence of these teachings by reading the book from beginning to end. But because the teachings are so interwoven, you might also open the book randomly to discover what, in any given moment, might bring some illumination into your life.

Some of the stories here are accompanied by an invitation to pause, reflect, and allow your own wisdom and understanding to awaken. These moments of going beyond the words and coming home to presence are the gateway to all true healing and freedom.

Even though the gold of your true nature can get buried beneath fear, uncertainty, and confusion, the more you trust this loving presence as the truth of who you are, the more fully you will call it forth in yourself and in all those you touch. And in our communities, as we humans increasingly remember that gold, we'll treat each other and all beings with a growing reverence and love.

*May we trust and live from the purity of
our boundless, radiant heart.*

*And may we hold hands as we awaken together,
bringing our shared caring*

*to this precious, troubled, mysterious,
and beautiful world.*

With loving blessings,

TRUTH

OUR BASIC GOODNESS

The gold of our true nature can never be tarnished. No matter how it might get covered over or disguised by feelings of anger, deficiency, or fear, our awareness remains radiant and pure. In the moments of remembering and trusting this basic goodness of our Being, the grip of "something's wrong" dissolves and we open to happiness, peace, and freedom.

WHAT IS GOOD ENOUGH?

I could have done that better. I should have gotten more done. I wish I had been more sensitive. For many years, "never enough" was a chronic habit of my mind, and I could run endless variations on the theme. Finally one night before going to bed, I sat down and asked myself: "Okay, what would be enough? What do I have to do to be *good enough*?"

Over the next weeks I started tracking what happened after I'd completed a successful weekend of teaching, or after receiving feedback about contributing to others' well-being, or after being particularly kind or generous with someone. The *enough* feeling would last for about 2.4 minutes before I'd start fixating on what else I needed to do, how I needed to prepare for the next event, how I needed to be more consistently sensitive and kind. Even the most satisfying accomplishments, upon close inspection, would seem tainted by ego, and therefore not *spiritual* enough. Whatever I was doing, it didn't leave me with an enduring sense of enough.

Since that long-ago evening when I faced the never-ending narrative of falling short, I have discovered that enoughness has absolutely zero to do with accomplishing, nothing to do with achieving, and is not at all about trying to be good enough. Rather, the realization of *enough* is right here in the fullness of presence, in the tenderness of an open heart, in the silence that is listening to this life. These are the moments when the glow of gold shines through.

REFLECTION Pause and let yourself sink into this moment, into presence, into your heart. Gently say to yourself, "There's nothing to do. This is enough . . . I am enough." Feel the fullness and peace of coming home.

THANK YOU FOR EVERYTHING

Hundreds of years ago in Japan, a Zen master named Sono was known far and wide for her wisdom. Many came to her to find healing for their bodies, their minds, their hearts. But no matter what their pain or affliction, Sono offered one simple remedy: "Every day repeat this mantra: 'Thank you for everything, I have no complaints whatsoever.'" As the story goes, those who took her advice to heart found happiness and healing.

One day when my son, Narayan, was an adolescent and caught up in grumbling and being dissatisfied with life in general, I told him the story about Sono, hoping it might offer some perspective. It didn't seem to make much of a dent. But not long after, on the way to an appointment with the dentist, we got caught in a lot of traffic. Our car was at a total standstill, and the minutes were ticking by. White-knuckling the steering wheel, I muttered, "Oh shit." Narayan reached over and nudged me. "Mom," he said with a superior "gotcha" smile. "Thank you for everything, I have no complaints whatsoever!" Ever since, when my inner complainer arises, I still sometimes hear my son's playful voice channeling Sono's wisdom.

THE SECOND ARROW

One day, it is said, the Buddha was talking to a group of his followers about our habit of being down on ourselves when something goes wrong, and how that only imprisons us in suffering. Noticing that one of the young men there looked puzzled, he invited him forward and asked, "If a person is struck by an arrow, is it painful?" Probably thinking that was a pretty obvious question, the student responded, "Well, yes it is."

Nodding, the Buddha went on. "And if that same person is then struck by a second arrow, would that be even more painful?" The student replied, "Yes, it would be."

The Buddha then explained: In life, difficulty naturally arises—things don't go as we wish, or we have an accident, or we get sick. "We can't always control that first painful arrow. However," he went on, "we can add to our pain by the way we react to what's happening." He added that we might feel victimized or angry about life being unfair, or we might blame ourselves for our poor self-care. "Our reaction is the second arrow, and it intensifies our suffering," said the Buddha. "We become

identified with a suffering self." The young man nodded, now understanding how painful the added emotional reactivity can be.

It's helpful to remember that the first arrow in this story is not only about that unpleasant feeling we experience when something goes wrong in our lives. The first arrow can also be the emotional pain we feel when we are afraid or angry, when we feel grief or hatred. It can be the pain of depression or lust. And when we then respond by blaming ourselves for these already painful feelings, we are shooting the second arrow. As we awaken compassion for ourselves and release shame and self-judgment, we free ourselves from this suffering and heal our hearts.

REFLECTION The next time fear or anger arises, try holding it with compassion rather than shooting the second arrow of painful self-judgment and blame.

RESISTING THE DEMONS

We are often at war with our painful emotions and bad habits, the unwanted shadow parts of ourselves. We try denying them and pushing them away; we try to hide them, fix them, or condemn them. It's typically a losing fight.

Milarepa, a twelfth-century Tibetan master, found himself in such a battle. After many years of living in solitude, doing practices in his mountain retreat, he returned one evening to find his cave filled with demons. Although he understood that they were just projections of his own mind, that didn't make them any less threatening or horrible. But how was he to get rid of them?

First, he thought teaching them spiritual truths might help. They just ignored him. Angry and frustrated, he ran at them, trying to push them out of the cave. Far stronger than he, they laughed at him. At last Milarepa gave up, sat down on the floor and said, "I'm not leaving, and it looks like you are not either, so let us just live here together." That's how we might finally respond to the especially stubborn demons we live with: "Well, that's just the way I am. I guess I have to live with it. This is just the way life is."

But to Milarepa's surprise, when he stopped resisting, instead of taking over, all the demons got up and left the cave. All except one, and this one was particularly powerful. Milarepa realized that the only thing he could do was have the courage to deepen his surrender. He walked over to that great demon and placed his head inside its gigantic mouth. "Just eat me up if you want to," Milarepa said. At that moment the demon vanished.

I have found that it is only when I stop resisting entirely—stop judging, stop trying to control, stop tensing against, stop avoiding—only then do I arrive in an open, tender, and healing presence. In that open tenderness, there's nowhere for the painful shadow energies to root. With true surrender of all strategies of self-protection, the demons lose their power. When the resistance is gone, so are the demons.

🌿 REFLECTION What is your worst demon? Is it fear? Shame? Hatred? Loneliness? What would it mean to surrender resistance and directly feel your feelings when this demon next arises?

THIS TOO

During the years I was living in an ashram, I went through periodic bouts of mistrust and anger at our spiritual teacher and felt guilty about not being a totally devoted student. At those times I felt that I didn't really belong to the community. I remember one morning during our group gathering for yoga and meditation when I was filled with angry thoughts about what was wrong with this teacher and with the ashram, but I also felt shame for all that negativity. I was fighting myself for fighting others in my world.

Some wise part of me whispered, "Let it all be here, let all these feelings belong." So each time the negative feelings arose, I sent the message "This belongs. This anger belongs. This shame belongs. This feeling of loneliness belongs." With whatever was arising, I thought, "This too . . . this belongs."

I wasn't saying that the angry judgments about myself or others were true. I wasn't saying that any of the feelings belonged forever. Nor was I dismissing the messages of my emotions. I was simply recognizing that, in these moments, all the waves arising in the ocean of my being belonged; they were a part of this life.

A profound shift happened inside me. By *not* trying to stop the waves, by allowing them to be there, I relaxed open. I was the ocean, including those waves. And in that wholeness I could sense again my inherent belonging to my own life, to all life.

Saying "this belongs" to my feelings didn't prevent me from listening to the intelligence of my emotional life and ultimately leaving the ashram. But instead of reacting from a place of victimhood, it allowed me to listen and respond from an awake, discerning presence.

🌿 REFLECTION Is there something going on in your life right now that brings up painful feelings? What happens if you send the message "this belongs" to the feelings that are arising? How might saying "this belongs," as a part of life, help you respond to the situation with more presence and creativity?

NEWSPAPER MEDITATION

During the weeks leading up to the 2003 invasion of Iraq, led by the United States military, I found myself increasingly agitated. Every day the news headlines were making it clear where all the talk by politicians was leading. I'd open the newspaper and find myself feeling anger and hostility toward those in government who were beating the drums of war. Just seeing their photos on the front page of the newspapers would set me off.

At the same time, my book *Radical Acceptance* had just come out, and students were asking me how acceptance and activism could go together. How could we "radically accept" and seek change at the same time? How could we see what was going on and not do something in response? I was increasingly aware that the hostility I was feeling in my own mind was actually another form of violence. And yet I needed to stay engaged; I needed to do something, to take some kind of action.

Since I wasn't going to stop reading the newspaper, I decided to make it into a meditation. Each morning I would open the paper, check out the headlines, read a few paragraphs . . . then pause.

I'd notice my reactions—the thoughts and feeling of outrage. I'd allow the experience to move in my mind and body, not denying or feeding it, just witnessing the response I was having to the latest reports.

I began to see that when I opened to the full force of the anger I was feeling, I could sense within it fear for our world. And as I opened to the fear, it unfolded into grief for the suffering and devastation that was inevitable in war. And out of the grief arose a deep caring for all the beings—humans and animals and trees—that would be harmed by the violence we were moving toward.

After a number of newspaper-meditation sessions, I had the opportunity to join others in Washington, DC, to protest the war. We were peacefully arrested—along with clergy of all denominations, Nobel laureates, and elders—all of us expressing our caring for everyone directly affected by this war: soldiers and families, Iraqis and Americans alike. We held with compassion the enormous suffering we knew would come. We held peace rather than violence in our hearts.

By holding my feelings of anger and frustration with "radical acceptance," I could find my way to the caring that gives rise to wise action. Acceptance of whatever arises in us in the present moment is not a passive act. Rather, this engaged, mindful presence allows us to respond to our world from our deepest compassion and wisdom.

REFLECTION When you find yourself angry in any situation, notice what happens if you pause and just allow yourself to notice the intensity of the thoughts and feelings. Can you sense the fears or hurts under the anger? And under that, can you feel the vulnerability and tenderness of your caring heart?

MEET YOUR EDGE AND SOFTEN

I'd been teaching, writing, exercising, trying to do everything I could as well as I could—and then one day my body crashed. I ended up flat out in a hospital bed with an IV drip stuck in my arm.

The first night there, feeling completely alone and helpless, I lay awake, my mind churning. *How much worse might this get? Will I ever be able to teach again? And what about writing? Will I even be able to sit at a computer and work? Is there anything in the future I can count on?* My life was out of my hands. Everything felt so fragile, temporary, and out of my control.

The words of a Tibetan teacher came to mind— the essence of spiritual practice is "to meet our edge and soften." I was at that edge, facing fear, aloneness, despair. How could I soften in the face of that? Gently I encouraged myself to go right into the painful edge of fear and soften there. As I allowed the fear, a deep, cutting grief arose, tearing at my heart. It was as if I were falling into a black hole of grief. It was like dying: *The life I have known might no longer be possible.*

"Just be there," I told myself, sobbing as grief surged through my body. With my hand on my heart,

I kept repeating, "Sweetheart, just soften . . . Let go, it's okay." The deeper the pain, the more tender my inner voice became. What followed was a full surrendering, and with that profound letting go at the edge, a space opened up inside me that was filled with the tenderness of pure love. Over the next moments I was surrounded, held, and suffused with a timeless loving presence.

"Sweetheart, just soften" became my mantra for the remainder of my hospital stay. I've since recovered fully, and yet I still can find myself feeling vulnerable and anxious about what's around the corner, fearful about failing in some way. When this arises, I sense that I've met an edge, and I gently invite myself to soften. With each round of facing the fear about what may come, a deeper trust can arise. Whatever my life might bring, I can practice meeting that edge and softening.

⤳ REFLECTION Is there an edge of fear you are standing at right now? Let yourself open to the fear or sorrow or grief, and allow yourself to meet that edge and soften. Notice what shifts as you offer a clear and kind presence to this vulnerable part of you.

THE GIFT OF A FAILED STRATEGY

One of my favorite practices is to intentionally focus on seeing the goodness in others—really seeing who is there. And one of the perfect places for me to keep this in mind is during my book-signing events. I sit at a table and greet each person holding out one of my books, front page open, waiting for a friendly note from me addressed especially to them. I like to pause with each person and take a moment to appreciate who is there in front of me.

However, although I can see someone I know and tell you about their past and their primary relationship—about where they are in their lives and how they get stuck—I often come up short when trying to remember their name!

This gets especially tricky when I'm in my home community. When *True Refuge* came out, I felt really tense about the book signing there, fearing that someone I knew very, very well would come up and hand me the book, and I would go blank with no idea of what their name was. I could imagine smiling and asking, "Who would you like me to address this to?" and them saying, "Oh, to me!"

And so I started this semi-devious strategy in which I would ask, "How do you spell your name?" I figured it's okay to be a bad speller but not to forget somebody's name, because remembering a name is part of what tells someone you appreciate them.

Well, there I was, doing the book signing, and a woman came up—a very, very dear person I have known for years—and of course I could not remember her name. It was as if my anxiety had created a self-fulfilling prophecy.

I pulled out my strategy. "How do you spell your name?" I asked innocently. And she said, "J-A-N-E." Busted. We both burst into laughter, and I told her about the issue I have with names. "You know," I said, "it has been my fear that someone named Bob would come along and I would say, 'How do you spell it?'"

We both laughed and thought that was pretty funny, but inside I was still feeling awful for forgetting her name. So wanting to do a very loving inscription to make up for it, I opened her book, and before I even knew it, I had written: "To Bob."

She still signs her emails to me: "Love, Bob."

I was the beneficiary of a failed strategy. Even though I'd tried pretending in hopes of controlling the situation, I had gotten exposed. And in that realness, my friend and I were brought closer.

When we are afraid or feeling inadequate in some way, our inner controller can take over and try to protect us with some little dissembling strategy. What a relief it can be to finally admit to our imperfections! Now, before book signings, my prayer to Bob (whoops, I mean God) is: "May I be real."

REFLECTION Are there situations in your life where you rely on some pretense to cover up a part of you that feels vulnerable or inadequate? What might it feel like to let go and "be real"?

FROM WHITE GUILT
TO HEARTBREAK

For three years, I was part of a small group of meditators from the Washington, DC, area who started meeting to deepen our understanding of what life was like for those from different group identities. We were Black, Brown, White, transgender, cisgender, gay, and straight. Our shared intention was to bring mindfulness and compassion to our journey together.

During our first few months, we shared our experiences as part of a dominant or nondominant population. Most who came from marginalized groups had endured daily violations, feeling discounted, invisible, and demeaned. Some reported a lifelong sense of fearing their body was in danger. One Black woman shared a childhood experience of witnessing her father's humiliation when he was pulled over and disrespected by police for no reason. A Black mother spoke of her fear for her teenage son whenever he was out at night. A gay man described relentless bullying in his youth. A transgender person told of the long painful years of keeping the truth from their parents.

As I listened to them share their vulnerability and watched the intimacy among them grow, I found myself increasingly aware that I had lived most of my life in a relatively safe and privileged White bubble. While for decades I've had friends and family who identify along the spectrum of gender and sexual orientations, my world—neighborhood, teaching, socializing—included few people of color. So when I tried to talk about my own experience as a White woman or offer a compassionate presence to those violated by racism, I felt stilted, self-conscious, and afraid of making an insensitive misstep. I ended up leaving each meeting feeling like an outsider.

One gathering that was held at my house turned out to be particularly disturbing for me. I saw how defensive, and then guilty, I felt about being White. I also saw how desperately I wanted to prove my worth as a White ally—and how much I wanted approval for that from people of color. This insecurity had now become an increasingly familiar feeling.

That day after everyone left, I stayed in the room where we had met and tried to untangle my emotions. I allowed the feelings to arise, and in a short time touched into an acute sense of being a bad person. I was White and I belonged to a race that was inflicting daily suffering on others. In my mind and, I imagined, in the eyes of many in the group, I was a "bad other." As I stayed with these feelings, the awareness of centuries of trauma perpetrated by White people against Black people felt like a crushing weight. Not only was I part of the problem, the deepest pain was feeling I wasn't doing enough to repair the damage.

I leaned into that, opening to the felt sense in my body of personal badness. It was a queasy, heavy, sore aching in my heart and belly, and then a deepening of powerlessness and despair. As I moved into the center of that suffering, what emerged was the raw pain of separation and the primal longing to belong.

As the longing grew more poignant and intense, something crumbled and broke open within me. Grief poured out for all the suffering that comes from making fellow humans "the Other," an object less human and valuable than ourselves. I grieved the violence and horrors of racism—my mind filled with images of lynchings, of children taken from enslaved parents, of enslaved couples separated, of the ongoing imprisoning, dehumanizing, and "keeping down" of Black people I knew and cared about. And I grieved for those of us from the dominant race—how our hearts and consciousness become numbed, dulled, and defended as we violate fellow beings; how we become imprisoned in an artificially divided, confined world.

As my mind quieted, I saw clearly that there was no "bad self," but rather a conditioned identification with a dominant group that had been fortified by centuries of racism. Like all of us in this society, I had internalized the messages of our racial caste system and the classifications of superior and inferior that maintain it. But I didn't have to be identified with or contracted by these beliefs and feelings. Resting in an openhearted awareness, it was possible to acknowledge and experience the pain of this conditioning without the judgment and self-aversion that comes from taking it personally. The grieving had broken my heart open, and that tender spaciousness could now hold our hurting world with compassion.

My experience that evening transformed my relationship with others in the group. I began to see and regard my patterns of White fragility—my guilt and defensiveness—with more clarity and kindness. The reactivity I still felt at times was painfully real, but it no longer felt as personal. I could more quickly return home to heartbreak and openness. This shift from guilt to sorrow and caring opened the way for loving connection with others and a deepening dedication to helping undo racism in all its forms.

As a White person, I've found it necessary to intentionally turn toward the suffering of racism again and again with a willingness to stay with the discomfort. A racial caste system violates the humanity of us all, and our freedom requires that we see and feel this directly. My prayer is that we let our hearts be broken open so that we can tend to this great centuries-old wound we all suffer, and that our caring moves us to actively engage in repairing our world. This is an essential part of the spiritual path and a gateway to truly living from love.

≫ REFLECTION How has the suffering of racism touched your heart and your life? When and how did you first become aware of "racial difference"? Have the messages of superior and inferior separated you from yourself and others? How might you deepen your attention and engagement in a way that would serve the healing of separation and the repair of our world?

If you want to realize who you really are and who others are, avoid making any living being better or worse than you, superior or inferior. And if your mind erects a hierarchy, don't believe it! In the moments of releasing comparisons, judgments, and hierarchies, we awaken to the Oneness that is the fabric of all Being and a reverence for the infinite and ever-changing expressions of life.

SPEAKING AND RECEIVING DIFFICULT TRUTHS

When Jonathan and I got married, my wedding vows to him included the bold aspiration expressed in a poem by Rainer Maria Rilke:

> *I want to unfold.*
> *Let no place in me hold itself closed,*
> *for where I am closed, I am false.*
> *I want to stay clear in your sight.*

Well, this has proven to be no small task. I had pledged myself to a path of intimacy that meant having the courage to be open and real about everything, including parts of myself I might want to hide.

One of the biggest tests of that marriage vow happened only two years after our wedding. I was suddenly facing chronic health problems that would clearly put an end to many of the activities we loved doing together—mountain hiking, biking, swimming, boogie boarding. I could see a future in which Jonathan remained healthy and athletic while I became less and less fit and desirable. I sank into a swamp of shame.

For weeks I hid these feelings—or hoped I did. I couldn't bear to let him see my shame and insecurity. But keeping those feelings to myself was toxic—I grew increasingly depressed and distant. Jonathan was confused and uneasy. I was imprisoned, closed down.

Finally one day I asked if we could talk. Jonathan readily admits that those words, "Honey, we need to talk," can elicit a feeling in him of "Oh god, I'm going to die!" And then his next thought typically is: "Okay, what did I do wrong now?" But that day maybe something in how shaky I felt made him do what his "good listener" does. He listened, making sure I was saying everything I wanted and needed to say. And then he mirrored back to me what I was saying, letting me know he understood. After it was clear to me that he had heard my fears that he would be stuck with an aging, sickly woman and that things could only get worse, he told me kindly and clearly that his love for me was not tied to boogie boarding or any other activity. He cherished our togetherness, unrelated to any of the particulars of what we could do.

And then I listened as he confessed feeling stuck in his own feelings of fear and impotence in seeing me so unwell, and how that pained and distanced him. As I held a tender space for that vulnerability, he too felt seen and loved.

Poet Adrienne Rich wrote: "An honorable human relationship, that is, one in which two people have the right to use the word 'love,' is a process of deepening the truths they can tell each other. It is important to do this because it breaks down human self-delusion and isolation."

As Jonathan and I keep practicing open communication, we rediscover over and over that no matter how much we might resist or fear being vulnerable, wanting to protect ourselves, it always turns out to be worth having taken the chance with each other. Through doing that, we come to trust the space of shared love and presence that holds our lives.

Believing we are separate selves is one of our deepest illusions and the source of our suffering. If we try to hide our feelings of unworthiness or unlovableness, we deepen the sense of separation from others. Taking the risk to be vulnerable and real reveals the truth of our belonging—to each other, to ourselves, to this world we share.

REFLECTION Is there a truth about your own vulnerability that you are holding back in an important relationship? Can you imagine, for the sake of deepening love, taking the risk of being more real?

NOT A PROBLEM

Joseph Goldstein was my first vipassana meditation teacher, and one of the things he said still regularly comes into my awareness. "Every time I think there is a problem," he said, "I decide there isn't one." I have found that simple guideline to be helpful in so many situations! When we label some situation as "a problem," we easily get caught inside our "small self." The mind tightens and we see things from only one perspective. But when we can let go of that negative frame, we can begin to unwind our stories and conclusions and start seeing a situation with a fresh perspective.

Some years ago my siblings and I were in a kind of dicey place, with some disagreements about financial workings around a property we inherited. We were all entrenched in our own individual views, each of us thinking: "Oh, this is a big problem!"

During this time, I had the opportunity to go on retreat. Outside the heat of the family conflict and in the quiet of the meditation hall, I found myself remembering Joseph's words. Thinking about the challenges my siblings and I were entangled in, I told myself: "I am going to decide this is not a problem anymore."

Every time the situation would come up in my mind, I would say, "Not a problem! It is unresolved, it is difficult, it is sticky, but it is not a *problem*!"

It was amazing. Just deciding that what we were facing wasn't a problem created a little more space in my way of thinking about it and a little less fixation on what had seemed to be intractable issues. After the retreat, when I returned to negotiations with my family, the greater ease and openness in my mind made a helpful difference.

Removing the frame of "problem" from the challenges that arise is not a delusional practice in which we diminish the experience of real suffering, see harm and turn away, or deny that situations can be hard to solve. Rather, it makes room for us to recognize more clearly what is happening without assuming life should be different and calling a situation "bad" or "wrong." We can then see things just as they are— with all their painful twists and tangles and also their potential for creative responses and deep awakening.

✎ REFLECTION Are you currently facing a challenging situation in some area of your life? If you let go of labeling it as "a problem," what possibilities open in your mind?

THANK YOU, SIRI

At least twice a week Jonathan and I meditate together in the morning. It's one of the rituals we are dedicated to as a couple. Part of this time also becomes a check-in—we talk about our lives, what we are grateful for, and where we feel challenged. We end by looking directly at our relationship and often use the inquiry: *Is there anything between you and me that keeps us from feeling connected right now?*

One particular morning, after we'd chatted for a while, Jonathan got up to leave, almost forgetting that last part of our check-in. I'd already been carrying a certain tension, a background of chronic complaint, because I felt like I was always the more curious one about the "What's between us" thing. I seemed to be the one who wanted to pay attention to whether there might be something that needed tending to. And he was usually ready to harmonize but not as interested in exploring those potentially edgy domains.

That morning I didn't have any current issue in mind, but I was carrying a grudge from something a few days before, and I wanted to put him on the spot. "So, how are *we* doing?" I asked him. To be sure I was framing the question in a positive and invitational way, I added nicely: "Is there anything we should be paying attention to?"

Then I sat back. I was on my turf; I was good at this kind of thing. Jonathan started squirming because he figured there must be something on my mind. He was afraid, of course, that he had missed something and I was going to pounce on it. He looked at me hopefully like I might give him a clue, but I was totally silent, just sitting there. Then he got that deer-in-the-headlights look, like, "Oh my gosh, something *is* really going on."

After a moment, a mischievous look came over his face. He pulled out his iPhone, tapped the screen, and said, "Siri, how do you respond when your wife asks, 'How are we doing?'" Within moments, he had an answer—and this is the absolute truth. Siri said, "You say: 'I am okay. You are okay. And this is the best of all possible worlds.'" I mean, what could I do? We had a good laugh and went out for a walk.

Once we were outside, I had to own the reactive space I'd been in and admit that what I'd done was a passive-aggressive move; it hadn't been well intended. I had wanted to make him uncomfortable. By my actually naming that—honestly naming the pattern—the two of us were able to find fresh ground with more trust and mutual willingness to look at what might be between us when something does come up. And whether or not something between us needs tending, we always know Siri has our back should we get stuck.

REFLECTION When you are feeling upset with someone you love, do you remember to ask Siri for help?

WHAT YOU PRACTICE
GROWS STRONGER

If you practice obsessive worry or blame, these pathways in your body and mind become deeply grooved and familiar. They imprison you in a small, tight, and endangered sense of self.

If you practice thoughts of gratitude, curiosity, and care, the ego-self becomes porous and your goodness easily shines through.

You can choose what you practice. Why not choose to cultivate the goodness and let the gold shine through?

REAL BUT NOT TRUE

The Tibetan teacher Tsoknyi Rinpoche offers a simple phrase that can be a liberating reminder: "Real but not true." It means that although the thoughts and feelings we are experiencing are real—they are really happening—their message and our interpretations are not the truth itself. At best, our thoughts and understandings are useful representations of reality. But because they are often fear-driven, they become distortions that can lead to suffering.

"Real but not true" has become a valued tool for me and for many students I work with. When I am caught in an unpleasant mood—irritated, anxious, or depressed—I ask myself "What am I believing?" Usually I find I've locked into some sense of being deficient, of falling short. Then I'll remind myself: Real but not true. Yes, these are real thoughts and real feelings, but is it really true that something's wrong with me? Even just the inquiry—"Is this really the truth? Might this be Real but not True?"—shakes the solidity of the belief. There's more choice; I don't have to believe the beliefs! Remembering this mantra offers space around the tight and fearful thoughts, just enough so I can find my way back to presence.

SACRED PRESENCE

I was about to give a talk on "sacred presence" and how when we multitask our attention is divided and we're unable to perceive the mystery and beauty of what is here and now.

So in the shower that morning, I was reflecting on what I would say about this when all of a sudden I realized I was slathering my hair with shaving cream. So much for sacred presence! "Okay," I thought, "I will never tell anybody this!" But here we are . . .

EVERY DAY, NO MATTER WHAT

During the twelve years I lived in an ashram, daily meditation practice was a given. It was the rhythm of my life, and I had the support of a regular schedule and others to practice with. It wasn't quite as easy after I left, but still some time for sitting every day was woven into my life.

And then my son, Narayan, was born. A predictable daily schedule was a thing of the past. I was exhausted from the demands of a newborn, and even finding time to take a shower was difficult, let alone the idea of spending time sitting quietly in silence.

One morning, after another night with too little sleep, I discovered that Narayan's father had forgotten to get something we needed when he went to the supermarket. I snapped at him, feeling overwhelmed at yet another thing to attend to. "Maybe you'd like to take a little time to meditate," he suggested in response. I immediately handed the baby over and fled to my little altar. The moment I sat down, I dissolved in tears. I missed this simple act of sitting for a few moments to remember. I missed, as the poet Rumi puts it, "making regular visits" to myself.

As I sat, breathing, just being, feeling the sun pouring through the window, hearing the sounds of my husband talking softly to Narayan, I made a vow to myself: Every day, no matter what, I will find a time to be still and present with whatever is happening inside me. It doesn't matter where or when or how long; it doesn't matter whether I am sitting or standing. Just every day.

And I have honored that pledge. These days I typically meditate for thirty to forty-five minutes in the morning, and then I do a shorter sit in the evening. But when Narayan was still little, it was sometimes hard to find more than a few moments at any time during the day. Sometimes, right before going to sleep, I'd sit on the edge of my bed for just three minutes, being present with the sensations and feelings moving through me. But that counted; it made a difference.

"Every day no matter what" is a gift to your soul, a gift of remembering. As Zen master Suzuki Roshi puts it: *The most important thing is remembering the most important thing.* Every day. The daily pause to just be present builds on itself and creates a gravitational field that increasingly calls you to presence throughout all the moments of your life.

LOVE

*The starting place of all healing is embracing even
the most painful and shameful parts of our inner
experience. Compassion for ourselves naturally leads
to caring about others and eventually unfolds into
an unconditional and inclusive love for life
we never imagined possible.*

LOVE IS ALWAYS LOVING YOU

Something a spiritual teacher once said has stayed with me for years: "Love is always loving you." While the phrase resonated immediately, my understanding at first was mostly conceptual. It only became a lived experience when I found myself in a deep hole of misery.

I had arrived at my annual winter retreat in New England after a really busy holiday season, so there was a lot of unwinding to do. As part of slowing down, I had to face some of my patterns of self-centeredness, insensitivity, and controlling that had been on display during the days spent with family. This meant that as soon as things quieted down inside, up came that tenacious sense of "bad personhood," a very familiar feeling that some core part of me was flawed. This time, the judging self seemed particularly harsh.

As I touched into the sensations and pain of these feelings, I contacted a younger version of myself, one that was deeply insecure and filled with self-hatred. I tried to hold this vulnerable place with compassion, but that didn't work. I tried all the things I knew how to do to remember my goodness, but that young part dug in her heels: "Something's really wrong with me, I can't change and it's not okay to be how I am." I started crying, despairing, helplessly sunk in believing "I am unloveable."

I let myself open to the fullness of that despairing part, and as I did, I could sense myself reaching out for help. The words came spontaneously: "Please love me." The whisper was coming from a place of broken-heartedness and deep, deep yearning. "Please love me," I whispered again and again.

Something in me knew what I was wanting—knew what the source of loving would be like, what the experience of being loved would feel like. My whispers were calling forth a luminous, warm, intimate presence that I could sense surrounding me, absolutely seeing and caring about me. Now, the realization of "love is always loving you," bathed every part of my being. As I opened to this, I actually felt a kiss of blessing on my brow. And with that, the small, tight self that had felt so unlovable was suddenly bathed in love, dissolving any sense of separation. I was merging with and becoming one with the light that surrounded and filled me. And then there was just a vast field of loving presence, aware of and tenderly holding the changing currents of sensations, feelings, and sounds.

This pathway of opening to loving awareness continues to infuse my lovingkindness practice. After sitting quietly for a few minutes, with a sincere heart I call on the light-filled, intimate, tender awareness that, even when forgotten, is truly here. I imagine and sense being blessed—sometimes with a touch or kiss to the brow—and am washed in loving, am dissolved into loving. Resting in that heartspace, I bring others to mind and offer them that caring blessing. The field of loving awareness becomes ever more boundless, tender, and vibrant.

LOVING OURSELVES INTO HEALING

Even after years of teaching and writing about self-compassion, I can still turn on myself, especially when I'm feeling stressed. In the middle of one busy day I noticed I was in a grim, humorless, bad mood. When I reviewed the day looking for a cause, I realized I had been in fight mode: negotiating a contract, grappling with a chapter due for a new book, pushing board members for a policy change. And my inner judge was condemning my uptight, irritated, combative self. "Why do I have to be like this? What's wrong with me?" I felt separate—in conflict with the world and myself.

It was this same pain of feeling deficient and disconnected that first led me to the spiritual path, and it continues to remind me to come into presence and soften my heart. Getting stuck in painful emotions brings me back again and again to an insight that has profoundly changed my life—self-compassion is essential to homecoming. I have to love myself into healing.

On that busy day when I was filled with self-judgment, I sat quietly for a few minutes, reminding myself to "Please be kind." When emotions are strong, my first step toward kindness is usually pausing, opening to the feelings, and telling myself "this belongs." It helped me that day to remind myself that there's nothing wrong with the arising of irritability, anxiety, or aggression. They are our limbic caretakers, our survival brain's primitive way of trying to protect and promote our well-being. Even self-judgment is well intended because it tries to improve us in ways that will make us more loveable and worthy.

Seeing those feelings as primitive forms of self-love helped me accept them as part of my human experience. And that acceptance was the beginning of loving myself into healing.

An allowing presence *is* the ground of love. As we then embrace the pain of our limbic caretakers with a tender heart, there is a profound and healing shift: The identification with an angry, judgmental, deficient self dissolves. It is clear that while emotions and stories will come and go, this loving awareness is the truth of who we are. Any moment of remembering this is a moment of true freedom.

REFLECTION When you find yourself stuck in self-judgment, pause for a few moments to honestly face the suffering of believing you are "not okay." Notice where you feel that suffering in your body. How it is arising in your mind? Then offer some gesture of kindness and understanding to these painful feelings—you might place your hand on your heart and softly whisper to yourself, "Please trust your heart." Or "Please be kind." Notice what happens when your intention is to love yourself into healing.

*By meeting pain with a tender presence,
we transform our wounds and losses
into fierce grace.*

THE BOUNDARY OF
OUR FREEDOM

On my first ten-day meditation retreat I had many opportunities to look closely at painful emotions and limiting beliefs. My mind was generating a barrage of self-judgments—from niggling little things like not packing comfortable pants to major failures as a parent—and I felt imprisoned in a deficient, separate self. It became clear to me that being at war with myself was cutting me off from my heart and perpetuating suffering.

I set the intention to accept rather than push away the underlying feelings of anxiety, fear, anger, and shame. Those precious moments of unconditional acceptance didn't last long at first, but always in them I discovered that my heart was open, caring, and free. Even when thoughts about the parts of myself I didn't like continued to come up, they were held with compassion, there was room for imperfection. My mantra became "The boundary to what I can accept is the boundary to my freedom."

Of course my negative judgments weren't restricted to my own personhood. I'd feel annoyed with people dear to me who weren't taking care of themselves in the way I thought they should. I'd get caught in judgments aimed at those who hold power and create suffering for vulnerable populations. But each time these thoughts arose, I'd remind myself that acceptance without boundaries meant including all beings in my heart. And I could feel how pushing anyone away created a wall that barricaded a small, separate self from others, from the world, from inner freedom. I could feel it in my tense body and constricted heart.

On that retreat I learned that when I shift my attention away from judging myself and others and let my heart open to the vulnerability we all share, the wall starts becoming more porous. As I open to that vulnerability with compassion, the light and warmth of my heart shines through freely. As Rumi puts it: "That hurt we embrace becomes joy. / Call it to your arms where it can change."

REFLECTION You might sit for three minutes with the simple intention to accept whatever experience arises inside you: changing thoughts, feelings, sensations, sounds. As you do, sense what you notice about the quality of your heart and your presence. Who are you in the moments of unconditionally accepting life?

When we feel held by a caring presence, by something larger than our small, frightened self, we begin to find room in our own heart for the fragments of our life, and for the lives of others. The suffering that might have seemed "too much" can awaken us to the sweetness of compassion.

LIVING TRUE TO OURSELVES

A hospice caregiver who had listened to the final reflections of thousands of dying people wrote an article that has remained with me for years. In it she said that the greatest regret she heard regularly from those at the end of their lives was: "I wish I'd had the courage to live a life true to myself."

Reading that, my thought was that it's not only the dying who have this regret. Many people feel an underlying disappointment about how they are living their lives. I started asking myself, "Am I living true to myself today? Right now?" This inquiry was so revealing and valuable that I began bringing it to my meditation students, asking, "Do you feel your life is aligned with what matters to your heart? Are you living true to yourself?"

Whenever we explore this together, students tell me things like, "Being true to myself means being loving and present and authentic." Some of them say it means being generous and serving those in need. For others, it's about expressing their creativity, believing in their own worthiness, or doing work they love. Some of them talk about having the courage to forgive and find reconciliation in difficult relationships or about engaging in actions that might be scary but are important in making a positive difference in the world.

Yet so often there is also an underlying self-doubt or questioning. They tell me that they regularly lose sight of their aspirations and get caught up in self-judgment and addictive behaviors. They go on autopilot or get stuck in painful old habits that distance them from others. One student said, "Each day there's a gap between my potential and how I live. That gap makes me feel like I'm always falling short."

Many times a day, I too notice that gap between my aspiration to live from loving awareness and the self-centeredness of my thoughts and actions. For years my negative judgments of myself fed what I now call the trance of unworthiness, the belief that I am a deficient self. But it's possible to break out of that trance. Now when I realize I've lost touch with my intention to be kind and present with others, I'm grateful for noticing rather than self-critical. Asking myself questions like, "In this moment, am I living from love?" reminds me of what's possible and calls me back into alignment with my true nature.

The longing to live true to ourselves is a natural and beautiful calling from our most pure and loving heart. Judging ourselves only distances us from this basic goodness. The real courage to live true to ourselves begins with holding our inner experience with compassion. This frees us to bring our light and love to all of life.

In the midst of our deepest emotional suffering,
self-compassion is the pathway
that will carry us home.

PLEASE, MAY I BE KIND

One of my favorite quotes is taped on a wall in my office: "To be kind, you must swerve regularly from your path." I need this reminder. Like so many, when I'm caught up in my busyness, trying to cross things off the list and on my way to somewhere else, I'm not so sensitive to opportunities to be kind. My attention is goal directed, and my heart can be tight.

A psychological study done at Princeton Theological Seminary revealed a lot about how this kind of narrow self-focus can get in the way of bringing compassion to our world. To look at the impact of time pressure on helpful behavior, the researchers told a group of seminary students that they would be crossing campus to a classroom where each would present a talk on the biblical parable of the Good Samaritan. As the students knew, in that story two important religious people pass right by a man on the street who clearly needs help. The only person who stops to assist him is someone who's considered a social outcast.

Some of the students were told they had just a few minutes to get to the classroom before the session for their talks would begin. Others were told they had enough time to get there on schedule. Then they were all sent individually on a route that would take them past a man (one of the researcher's associates) who was slumped in a doorway, coughing and obviously in need of help. Despite the fact that they were all on their way to present a talk about the Good Samaritan, only 10 percent of the students in the time-pressured group stopped to offer help. More than half (63 percent) of those in the group that was less hurried did stop.

I share this study frequently because our world desperately needs us to take care of each other, and swerving from our scheduled paths is not something we easily do. Focusing on our own concerns and stress can put us in a trance, covering over our natural sensitivity and compassion.

Over the years I've found a daily practice that helps my heart wake up from this goal-oriented trance. Each morning at the end of my meditation, I pray to remember throughout the day to be kind. Sometimes I simply whisper, "Please, may I be kind," and I often scan to see whom I might be in touch with that day so I can stay attuned to kindness when I'm with them. At the end of the day, I reflect back to see if I was openhearted with others. There is a sense of gladness when I see that I was. And when I realize the times I didn't swerve to be kind, I am accepting of this with compassion and with gratitude that I noticed. This allows me to then deepen the resolve that my heart may continue to awaken.

REFLECTION Can you recall situations during this past week where you did swerve from your path to be kind? Situations where you *wish* you had swerved? You might ask yourself every morning: "Today, what will help me remember to be kind?" And then check in each evening, reviewing the day with self-compassion, to support the awakening of your heart.

NARAYAN'S ANT FARM

When my son, Narayan, turned six, I gave him a gift that I knew would feed his curiosity about the natural world. Called an ant farm, this "kit" provided a view into the activities of living ants. Fascinated, he watched for hours. He named several and followed their efforts as they hurried back and forth, digging a network of tunnels and carrying food to store away. Watching the ant farm together became part of our daily ritual.

One day a few weeks later, Narayan arrived home from school deeply upset. On the playground some of the kids had made a game of stepping on ants. He was horrified that they could be hurting, even killing, some of these amazing creatures that he had come to know and admire.

We sat down together, and I held him as I explained that his friends didn't have ant farms so they hadn't had a chance, like he did, to get to know what ants are really like. I told him that when we pay attention to any living beings, we get to see how they move and relate to each other, how they are hungry, and what they are looking for. We find out that they are real and that, like us, they want to stay alive. As he listened intently, I told him that if his classmates ever paid really close attention to ants, they wouldn't hurt them anymore. Narayan turned to me and said, "I want to have them all over, so they can meet my ants."

The great spiritual teacher J. Krishnamurti taught that if we are truly paying attention, we are expressing love. When we pause and remain present with any part of this living world—the person we're with, the tree in our front yard, a squirrel perched on a branch—we allow our hearts to open and be touched by life. With loving attention, the living energy all around us becomes an intimate part of who we are.

WE ARE FRIENDS

During my morning walks I usually wander along the nearby Potomac River. Ducks and geese gather there in the shallows, and I often watch quietly as they paddle slowly around, dipping under for food and keeping company with each other. Each one has a distinct personality, and those in pairs have a clear bonding and loyalty. It's especially delightful to see the babies in the springtime, exploring a new world under the protective eye of their parents.

One year as I was walking in late fall, I heard the jarring report of guns firing upriver. As shock waves passed through my body, I realized the shots must be coming from hunters killing waterfowl. I felt flooded by the contrast between the innocence and powerlessness of these birds and the horror of their lives being destroyed. Those ducks and geese had become my friends. This was their home, and now they were being killed, most likely for recreational hunting. I started weeping as I imagined the confusion and fear of these beautiful creatures and their grief at the loss of a mate. My heart and mind railed at this violation: these beings are real, they feel, they are my friends!

As I headed back home on the trail along the river, I began to reflect on that sense of friendliness I felt with so much of this living world. Trotting beside me was k.d., my dog. My friend. Nearby, two cardinals were flitting around in some bushes. My friends. As I passed by a great sycamore hanging over the river, I paused and whispered, "You too are my friend." And just in affirming, I knew it was true. My mind went to animals around the world—pigs, chickens, cows, and more—who are thought of only as human food and whose lives are short, unnatural, and tormented. These, too, I thought sadly, are my friends. No matter who came to mind—human or nonhuman, my heart's response was, "We are friends." Each mattered, was precious, was part of me.

Along with the wash of sorrow still flowing through me came a sweet sense of belonging to a world of living beings who are not objects for our enjoyment or consumption but, like us, are aware and feeling. As I opened to that shared aliveness and sentience, I realized with a surge of gladness that *I am never alone*. Not in any way separate from all of life. With the knowing that "We are friends," invisible threads of connection had come alive in a sacred way, and I could feel the peace of being embedded in life itself.

REFLECTION The next time you walk outside, you might try an experiment. When a living being draws your attention—a dog, squirrel, bird, tree, insect—pause and say to yourself gently and sincerely "We are friends." Notice if your heart opens to the truth of your connectedness.

REVERENCE FOR LIFE

One spring I was leading a retreat in the Blue Ridge Mountains at a meditation center located near a dairy farm. In the silence of our early-morning sittings, we could clearly hear the cows lowing in distress. When I asked residents from the center why the cows were crying out, I was told that in the meat and dairy industry, farmers routinely separate calves from their mothers, usually immediately after birth. This allows the milk that would be available for the baby to be directed to human consumption—as well as making the cow ready for her next pregnancy cycle. Knowing that all mammals have a deep mother-child attachment, I well understood why cows can grieve for their calves for months.

As I listened to those crying mothers every morning, I imagined the terrible pain of separation they and their babies were going through. Others on the retreat were feeling the same. So we decided to include the cows and calves in our afternoon heart meditations. After quieting with the breath, we'd first bring to mind our own hurts, fears, and losses and would offer compassion to ourselves.

Then we'd open our hearts and awareness to others who might be in pain and facing difficulty, including those nearby mothers and calves. Sensing their pain and loss with tenderness, we'd offer our prayers that they be free of suffering.

In our contemporary world we are conditioned to value some beings more than others and certainly to consider human animals as more valuable than nonhuman ones. Yet this creation of hierarchy separates us from the living web of life and constricts and numbs our hearts. We awaken to our interconnectedness by attending to the vulnerability of all creatures and to our shared sentience and love for being alive. We are made of the same elements, all from the same mysterious source. Realizing this mutual belonging, our hearts awaken with care and respect for all living beings.

This can have a radical impact on how we live our lives. For increasing numbers of people, myself included, becoming aware of the enormous suffering caused by factory farming has led to choosing a plant-based diet. And for many of us, understanding the connection between eating animals and global warming has clarified that moving toward a plant-based diet is also key to healing our

Earth. In my own life, remaining aware of why I choose not to eat animals or their byproducts and consciously feeling gratitude for the plants I eat brings a deep healing sense of belonging to this precious world.

🌿 REFLECTION Are there animals who are in some way threatened or suffering that you feel particularly connected with? Maybe dogs abandoned in shelters, animals being raised for slaughter, or gorillas or elephants threatened by poachers and habitat loss. Allow yourself to get "close in" by imagining what life might be like for those animals. Sense how they, like you, want to live their lives fully and freely. Then offer your heartfelt prayer for their relief.

*In the safe haven of belonging to others, we can begin
to discover the sanctuary of peace that dwells
within our own being.*

OUR SECRET BEAUTY

When I teach lovingkindness meditation, students sometimes stay after class and let me know how healing it was to reflect on the goodness of their loved ones. After one such class, I was so moved by what I heard that I decided to ask my friends on Facebook to write about their experiences of seeing the basic goodness in others. What arose was a wonderful, heartwarming sharing! Parents talked about the curiosity and wonder in their children, partners offered vignettes about each other's playfulness and generosity, a few people told stories of witnessing the wisdom and selflessness of their elderly parents, and several wrote about receiving kindnesses from people they didn't know.

It happened that my birthday came up not long after that sweet exploration. Inspired by my Facebook invitation, a dear friend sent me a greeting card with a list of the ways she saw that basic goodness in me. This deep expression of her love brought tears to my eyes. As her generous words touched my heart, I was filled with awareness of *her* basic goodness, and I opened to the vast, loving heartspace we share together.

The experience reminded me of something I had read from the Trappist monk Thomas Merton. In his book *Conjectures of a Guilty Bystander*, Merton tells the story of a profound realization he had one day. It was not during prayer or in the monastery but on a busy street corner in Louisville, Kentucky, when he was suddenly flooded with the sense that he loved everyone around him. "They were mine and I theirs," he writes. His description of what he felt is one of my favorite quotes about the possibility of truly cherishing each other:

> *I suddenly saw the secret beauty of their hearts, the depth of their hearts where neither sin nor knowledge could reach, the core of reality, the person that each one is in the eyes of the divine. If only they could see themselves as they really are. If only we could see each other that way all the time. There would be no more war, no more hatred, no more cruelty, no more greed. I suppose the big problem would be that we would fall down and worship each other.*

If we can see beyond the changing moods, behaviors, and personalities of those who share our lives, we will recognize the light of awareness that is their essence. What a joy to pause and behold that basic goodness and to see how it shines through each of us as compassion, intelligence, aliveness, and creativity. In the moments of seeing that secret beauty, we fall in love with all of life.

THE BRIDGE BETWEEN
LONGING AND BELONGING

Growing up Unitarian meant learning to take in all views with a reasonably open mind. We'd playfully say that Moses had "received the Ten Suggestions." And when it came to prayer, the joke was to address "To whom it may concern." So I was pretty much left to figure out for myself what praying was actually about.

Through the decades, my relationship with prayer has emerged and deepened during encounters with grief, shame, fear, and despair. As I learned to sustain a real presence with those feelings, the pain of separation they revealed would unfold into deep sadness and longing. Over time, my yearning became increasingly clear: it was to belong to and be held by a larger source of love and presence. In the moments when this yearning overflowed, I'd reach out to what felt like an intimate and luminous field of sentience suffused with tenderness and caring. It felt like reaching out to the Great Mother of the Universe. I'd find myself first bathed in light and love and, increasingly over time, dissolved into that beloved presence.

Now, when there's a sense of being caught in a limited self, I often turn with a prayerful heart toward that larger source of loving awareness. As poet John O'Donohue wrote so beautifully, "Prayer is the bridge between longing and belonging." Prayers of longing soften the solidity of self. They create a porousness, a receptivity to the loving presence that is always available to us, whether we remember that or not. When we become humble, undefended, and available, we are open to directly knowing our belonging to that love.

I like to imagine prayer as a tree that is rooted deeply in the soils and rocks of our vulnerability, of our hurts and fears. The roots support the tree's limbs as they reach out with great longing and receptivity to the heavens. Our willingness to deeply touch our earthly vulnerability is what gives uplifting power to our prayer.

Prayer is a creative experiment for each of us, as we find the words and postures and images that make us available to the healing presence of love and grace. And what might feel like an empty ritual in one moment might deeply open us at another time. Words can be a mental whisper or said aloud. For some, the gesture of placing palms together at the heart and bowing the head increases a sense of openness, tenderness, and receptivity. And for some, a full prostration is an act of humble request and surrender. For myself, I'll bow my head slightly, and although I usually place my palms together, sometimes I'll raise cupped hands, as if offering whatever is here into a larger and loving presence. Through all these gestures, we are communing with a boundless field of love that is calling us home. And in time, like a river releasing itself into the ocean, we release ourselves into a larger belonging.

REFLECTION When you feel a sense of separation and longing, is there a gesture of prayer and some simple words that might open you to love and belonging? You might explore right now what happens if you simply bring your palms together and bow your head. Softly whisper your prayer, asking for love from the source you feel most deeply connected to.

KEEPING COMPANY WITH GRIEF

A friend of mine lost both of her parents within one year. Deeply bereft, she got in touch to ask if we could have a face-to-face talk on Skype. She had been quite close to her family and was the live-in caretaker during her parents' final months. It was such a huge loss for her that before the call I prayed that I could be deeply present.

I listened quietly as she told me about her parents and their last days. In the face of loss and grieving, there is often no right thing to say, but I was leaning in, getting ready to offer what I hoped would be most comforting and helpful. When she paused, I sensed she was waiting for me to speak, yet something inside me said, "No, wait." There was a bit of awkwardness as we sat in silence, looking at each other on the screen, but I knew I had to continue to trust the moment. And then something shifted: as we remained there simply present with each other, our tears started flowing, and we just sat together, crying.

When we are present with another's loss, we don't have to say or do anything in the moment other than open our heart and share that pain and sorrow. Sufi master Pir Vilayat Inayat Khan offered a profound understanding of what it really means to be with suffering. He said, "Like the Mother of the World who carries the pain of the world in her heart, each one of us is part of her heart and is, therefore, endowed with a certain measure of cosmic pain. You are sharing in the totality of that pain."

Offering companionship in pain acknowledges that suffering is living through all of us, and in our togetherness we enlarge the heartspace that can hold it with compassion. We become the Mother of the World, carrying the pain of the world in our heart.

The love and understanding of a friend,
like a deep well of the purest water,
refreshes the very source of our being.

OUR WORLD'S FEAR

I was meditating on a rock by the Potomac River when the reality of the coronavirus pandemic struck me fully for the first time. My heart clenched as I realized the likelihood that my pregnant daughter-in-law, who works at a hospital in San Francisco, could contract the virus and then spread it to her family: my son, granddaughter, and ex-husband who lives with them. My thoughts went to my many friends who are older or otherwise physically vulnerable, and to those who, due to race and/or being economically underprivileged, would bear the brunt of suffering. I thought of the inmates stuck in virus-infected prisons and of those packed into refugee camps around the world and on our own borders. With the spiraling currents of thought, my agitation spiked, and I found myself caught in the feelings of a scared, powerless, separate self.

Thankfully, the RAIN meditation, which I practice regularly, started spontaneously in my mind. I *Recognized* the feeling with a mental note: "Fear, fear." I *Allowed* the feeling, gently whispering to myself "This too belongs. This fear is not an intruder that shouldn't be here." Now, present, I could pause and deepen my attention. *Investigating*, I looked for where the sensations of fear were strongest in my body. It was a strangling feeling in my heart—a squeezing, aching hollow. Homing in to sense "What is this feeling really like?" I placed my hand on my heart. Breathing with the fear, I located the very epicenter of the pain, the raw edge of a pulsing, aching hollowness. Surrendering all resistance, I opened fully to the waves of fear as they arose and passed. I could feel my heart opening to ask what this deep vulnerable place most needed. What was it asking for? The answer that came was "to feel love . . . to feel belonging to something larger." Offering *Nurturing*, my attention opened wide to the field of love and awareness that is our very universe. As I imagined love pouring into me from that vast yet very intimate presence, I could feel it bathing and saturating the fear in my heart.

I sat in stillness after the RAIN, simply resting in the field of loving presence. Fear was still there, though being held by love, it was notably less intense. More significant: it no longer felt like "my" fear about the virus and all those affected by it.

Rather it was *the world's fear* that was being held in a vast and tender awareness.

And now, along with the currents of fear, I also opened to the aliveness surrounding me. I could hear the calling of the geese and the sound of the river flowing past the rocks below me. The suffering in the world that called my heart was real, and so was the wild beauty of this life.

Before the pandemic, there were times when we felt the reality of fear, loss, and grief, and we will continue to do so when this crisis has passed. We can know that the secret to healing is feeling the pain fully and bathing it in love. In those moments, painful feelings become the world's pain, and we become loving awareness itself.

REFLECTION When you are caught in difficult emotions, the RAIN meditation can bring you back to a wise and compassionate presence. Give yourself a few moments to pause and turn inward.

R **Recognize** what is happening. Mentally whisper whatever you are aware of: fear, anger, hurt, shame.

A   **Allow.** Let whatever you are feeling be here, without judging it, trying to fix it, or ignoring it. Simply pause and "let be." You might whisper "This too belongs."

I   **Investigate.** With curiosity, feel into your body—your throat, chest, belly. Discover where the emotions live inside you. You might gently place a hand wherever feelings are strongest. Sense what is needed or being asked for right now. Is it love? Forgiveness? Acceptance? Understanding?

N   **Nurture.** Offer care to feelings of vulnerability, hurt, or fear. Let the touch of your hand be tender, and send whatever message might most offer healing. You can imagine this coming from your own awake heart or from another being (friend, grandparent, spiritual figure, dog) you trust and love.

After the RAIN: Take some moments in stillness, simply sensing the quality of presence that has unfolded. Notice the shift from when you started (an angry or fearful or victimized self) to the compassionate awareness that is always here.

LOVING LIFE NO MATTER WHAT

I waved as the cars packed with friends and family pulled out of the driveway and headed for the beach without me that year—for the first time since I was a child. For as long as I could remember, summer meant Cape Cod with its piney woods and wide sandy beaches, our house filled with friends and our growing family as spouses and new children joined us. Whatever difficulties I might have been carrying in my heart were all held by the blissful hours we spent every day on the beach, riding the waves, swimming and floating out beyond the breakers, laying out on the hot sand to rest.

This summer it would be different. After years of mysteriously declining mobility and health, the diagnosis had come through—I had a genetic disease affecting connective tissues. The only known treatment was painkillers, and very gradually building muscle strength to stabilize my joints. I didn't know what my future would look like or whether I might ever again walk on the sandy beach with my family or play in the ocean with friends. I felt deeply alone, separate now from so much I loved. As tears of grief fell, a prayer arose in me: "Please, please may I find a way to peace. May I love life no matter what."

As I sat on the deck repeating that prayer of longing, my heart opened and opened until the grief turned into a pure, tender loving of life itself, no matter what might unfold. At that moment I knew most deeply that I could lose everything I cared about and that love would always be here, a timeless essence of my heart. Over the ensuing years I have gratefully found my way back to a surprising level of health and physical activity. Still, I know that everything I hold dear will eventually go—except this loving awareness that cherishes our ever-changing life.

FREEDOM

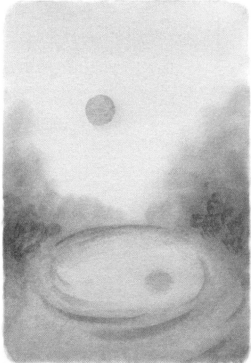

TWO WINGS

Like the two wings of a bird, Wisdom and Love are inseparable expressions of our natural awareness. The wing of Wisdom is our clear understanding of Truth, the nature of reality. The wing of Love is our capacity to respond to whatever we experience with a tender, caring, and appreciative heart. As we open these two wings of awareness, they carry us to the freedom of our awakened Being.

A SUNLIT SKY

For the next fifteen seconds, try *not* to be aware . . . starting now.

If you tried that, what happened? What did you notice?

When I give talks on the nature of awareness, I often invite people to try this short exercise. Then I ask how many were successful. There's usually a little laugh of acknowledgment in the room. I love this simple exercise because it makes so clear that awareness is always present—even when we are not conscious of it.

You might pause here for a few moments and check it out again: try *not* to be aware, and notice what happens.

Now, for a few seconds turn your attention directly toward awareness itself. What is awareness? Explore with interest and curiosity, not the objects of awareness—sounds, feelings, images—but awareness itself. What do you notice?

According to the teachings of Tibetan Buddhism, awareness is open, wakeful, and spontaneously responsive. Lacking form, center, or boundary—or any owner or inherent self—awareness is the open, allowing space in which all existence arises and dissolves. Although empty itself of "thingness," awareness is alive with wakefulness—the capacity to recognize the changing flow of sounds, sensations, smells, visual impressions. And awareness relates to this changing flow, including the infinite diversity of temporary living forms, with warmth or tenderness. This unlimited capacity for responsiveness includes love, compassion, joy, appreciation, and the many other qualities of heart.

These three qualities of awareness—open, wakeful, and tender—are integrated and inseparable. We might best understand them by likening them to a sunlit sky. There is no way to separate the light (wakefulness) from the open space it illuminates; there is no way to separate the warmth (tenderness) we feel from the shining light of the sun. They are inextricable expressions of a whole. And as Tibetan Buddhism teaches, this open, wakeful, tender awareness is the essence of our original and true nature. As we learn to turn our attention toward this awareness, as we learn to rest in it, we increasingly embody those qualities and live from the purity and fullness of who we really are.

REFLECTION Pause for a few moments and notice the changing flow of sounds, images, feelings, and sensations. Now become aware in the background, of the awareness that is here. Relax back and rest in awareness, *being* awareness itself. Can you sense the openness, the boundless and allowing space of presence? Can you sense the wakefulness, the quality of knowing? The tenderness or warmth in response to whatever arises?

"THIS IS IT"

True happiness arises out of simply being present in this moment, not grasping after anything, not wanting life to be any different from what it is, right now. There are countless opportunities for such moments of presence in our lives, when we are not leaning into the future or resisting what's here. Moments when we are letting life be just as it is. Opening to these moments is a taste of freedom.

When Jonathan and I are walking in nature, we often pause to take in the wonder of our surroundings, and also of our togetherness. At these times, one of us might say, "This is *it*," meaning this moment is all we have . . . and it's precious. The other will then good humoredly say, "No wait. THIS is *it*." And on we might go for several rounds, proclaiming that this—and then *this*—very moment is sacred. Along with the lightheartedness is a poignant reminder: When we intentionally stop the perpetual tumble into the future, we realize that what we cherish is only found in the Now. Truly, "This *is* it."

REMEMBERING THE WAY HOME

The Sufi poet Rumi is quoted as saying, "What comes into being gets lost in being and drunkenly forgets its way home." As part of the human journey, we each forget the vastness and depths of our awareness and love and become increasingly identified with a limited body and mind. Donning masks to hide the pain of unmet needs and to defend our vulnerability, we further narrow our sense of who we are. We wear the disguise of "busy important person," "angry victim," "deficient person," or "obsessed, addicted person." Sometimes it's depressed person. Or anxious person. Superior person. Loser. Most of us have a whole closetful of assumed personas. They might help us survive some challenging times, but the problem is we become identified with our masks and we end up believing that these false images are who we really are.

Just as it is a natural part of the human journey to put on these masks and get lost behind them, it is also part of our evolutionary unfolding to wake up to the fact that we are caught in a mistaken and confined identity. Sooner or later, slowly or quickly, we come to see that we've been living in

a trance, attached to a cluster of familiar masks that keep us believing we are separate and deficient. Courageously attending to the suffering of this trance awakens our longing to reconnect with the basic goodness we have always intuited is here. That suffering and longing are our own awareness, calling us home to our full intelligence, sensitivity, and love.

As we listen and dedicate ourselves to deepening presence, we see past the masks and discover behind them the beauty and freedom of our true nature.

REFLECTION What masks have you taken on to protect yourself on your journey? Who would you be if you no longer believed your most familiar mask is who you are?

SURRENDERING AGAIN
AND AGAIN

Some years ago when I was becoming well known as a teacher in the meditation world, I found myself in a painful dilemma. Along with the increased attention and recognition from others arose ego inflation, a subtle sense that I knew more than others and was the spiritually evolved one—the one with the answers. Often after a class or workshop, I'd come home and realize how that assumption of superiority and self-importance had separated me from others and from my own heart. And I'd sink into a mix of disappointment, sadness, and shame.

I decided I needed to release this "Special Person" inside me who was interfering with my relationships and with living in authentic presence. So I set my intention to amp up mindfulness. Whenever *She* appeared—after giving a talk, when reading thank-you notes from students, on hearing I'd be teaching to a full house—I'd pause and attempt to bring mindfulness and compassion to the thoughts and feelings moving through me. Sometimes I'd coach myself to "Let go, let go."

But it turned out that this only upped the ante: being on the lookout and trying to release Special Person made it even more evident how much she occupied my psyche. And with that, my shame increased—and my aversion. This inner persona was between me and freedom; she was keeping me hooked to an inflated, false sense of who I was. I urgently wanted to extricate myself from her clutches. (You can probably hear just how trapped in aversion and reactivity I was, but in my mind I was nobly endeavoring to wake up!)

One night at home, I was meditating by my altar, and as I quieted, a glow of light and feelings of peace began to emerge. And then there she was. Thoughts about an upcoming teaching event arose, and I was back inside that important, in-demand person. In desperation, I could hear an inner voice cry out, "What else can I do? I'm trying so hard, but this self-centeredness won't fade!"

At that point I finally got it. "*I* can't do this. *I* can't make part of the self go away. The self can't surrender and let go of the self! That's not its job." Willing myself to let go was only strengthening the inflated self. A gentle voice inside me whispered, "Stop. Just stop." Stop the war on myself.

Stop all the efforting. Stop trying to fix myself. And in taking a pause from all the "doing," my whole being began to lighten and open.

One of my favorite teachings about this pathway of true surrender comes from a story about Ananda, the Buddha's attendant and deeply devoted disciple. After the Buddha's death, when the great council of his enlightened followers was planned, Ananda was not invited. Although he had worked at it strenuously for years, he himself was not yet enlightened. And so on the eve of the council meeting, Ananda sat down to meditate, determined to practice vigorously all night, not stopping until he had attained full enlightenment. But after many hours, he was only exhausted and discouraged. In spite of all his effort, there had not been even the slightest progress. Toward dawn, Ananda decided to let go of striving and simply lie down and rest for a while. As the story goes, the moment his head touched the pillow, he was enlightened.

What freed Ananda? The release of all striving. Letting go. Simply resting in presence.

Certainly he had prepared the ground for awakening through many years of practicing meditation, learning to wake up out of his thoughts and open his heart. But it wasn't until all "doing" was surrendered and Ananda relaxed back into the awareness that is always and already here, that he realized freedom.

That night by my altar, it was the letting go that was freeing. But it wasn't a matter of the self letting go of ego, it was the *ceasing of all effort*. That sacred pause, those moments of nondoing, naturally filled with tender presence. And as that openhearted presence deepened and widened, the contractions of self dissolved into that larger, loving belonging.

Of course at some point my mind noticed, "Look what I did; I surrendered and am free of this." Special Person was trying to make a comeback. With an inner smile, I again heard that gentle whisper, "Stop. Just stop." And with that pausing came another round of softening and releasing into boundless, loving presence.

We can't *will* surrendering. Our wisdom knows that the pathway is surrender; our mind can be quiet and present, and our heart can be willing and prayerful. And yet, it is awareness that does the work. In the light and tenderness of awareness, thoughts naturally dissolve, bodily resistance softens, emotional fears and grasping unwind and release. Awareness illuminates its own presence, the mysterious truth of what we are. This realization might occur suddenly, as with Ananda, or unfold more gradually, which is my story. Either way, it is not "I" who does the surrendering. Rather, the tangles of a self-sense naturally release in the light of open, tender, nondoing presence.

Presence is the portal to everything we cherish.
And the pathway to this natural awareness is
simply relaxing back—resting in what is.

TOUCHING PRESENCE

We have all touched the intimacy of true presence. It might have been in the moments before sleep when you became still and relaxed, or when you paused to listen to rain on the roof. You may have touched presence while gazing in wonder at a star-filled sky. Maybe it was when you felt filled with gratitude after receiving someone's unexpected kindness. Or perhaps at those unforgettable passages of birth or death. In those moments, past and future recede, thoughts quiet, and there is the sacred sense of being right here, right now, awake and aware.

SAYING YES

On one of my first meditation retreats, I was sick with a sinus infection and struggling with the guilt and fear that the recent separation from my first husband was bringing up in me. I was swimming in negativity, in full reaction to the physical discomfort and emotional pain. Seeing how entrenched I was in resisting my experience, I decided to whisper "yes" to whatever I was feeling.

At first the yes was mechanical . . . and slightly entertaining, especially when it came to saying yes to a constant runny nose. But after doing this for a few hours, I started noticing more space in my mind around whatever was arising. And then slowly that space began to fill with tenderness. I could see that those inner weather systems of aversion and reactivity were arising and passing away on their own. They weren't targeting me or happening because of me, they were just part of the nature of life, playing out in this body and mind. Saying yes, letting them be, revealed the skylike awareness this changing weather was passing through—the wakeful and compassionate awareness that could hold it all.

By saying yes, I don't mean condoning anyone's harmful behaviors or accepting and believing the contents of our thoughts ("I'm a failure"). Rather, saying yes is an honest and courageous acknowledgment of what we are actually experiencing. This liberating attitude opens us into presence, and it allows us to respond to this moment with our full intelligence and compassion.

Each time you say yes to what's arising inside you, you deepen trust in the gold of your intrinsically openhearted awareness. You strengthen your confidence that you can meet whatever arises. This is inner freedom: rather than tensing against whatever may be next, you can open the gates and let the ten thousand joys and sorrows move through you.

REFLECTION Is there something challenging or difficult going on in your life right now? You might ask yourself, "What is the worst part of this situation? And what am I believing about it?" Bring your attention fully to the sensations in your body and to your feelings. Say yes to whatever is arising inside you—the unfolding hurts, anger, fear. Yes to the reality of your experience in the moment. Notice what happens during these moments of truthful acknowledgment and of courageous, openhearted presence. Can you imagine saying yes and embracing your entire imperfect and messy life?

THE UNREAL OTHER

Getting stuck in traffic can be a setup for losing mindfulness. I used to get really reactive driving during Washington, DC's notorious rush hour—especially when the person in front of me was going more slowly than I would like or the driver behind me was tailgating. So I began the practice of coming up alongside the car (if I could) and looking inside to see who was at the wheel. This was a kind of wake-up practice: when I could actually see the faces of the drivers, they'd become more real to me—fellow humans—and my annoyance would fade.

One day I was late for a meeting, and there was a car in front of me going very, very slowly. I became really bothered that this old Buick was plodding along below the speed limit, and all kinds of stereotypes were circling in my mind about the driver. He must be ancient. She's probably yakking with someone and not paying attention. I was completely into making that driver, whoever they were, an "unreal other." I engaged my strategy, pulling into the lane next to the car . . . and had the most jarring experience. This was about a year after my

dad died, and when I glanced over at the driver, he looked just like my father. In a single moment I went from irritated to weeping.

In that instant, the "unreal other" driving that Buick became a being to me—someone worthy of love and care. This incident deepened my commitment to staying awake whenever I was feeling stressed and making others unreal. I realized that in any moment when someone seems to be "in my way," I can pause and deepen my attention. This will allow me to see instead a being with a heart and with consciousness, and then the armoring that creates separation can soften.

THE VAST SKY OF AWARENESS

One of my favorite images to illustrate awareness comes from a Tibetan Buddhist teacher. In one of his classes, he drew a V shape on a big white sheet of paper. "What do you see?" he asked. "A bird," they all readily responded. "No," he said, "It's a sky with a bird flying through it."

We habitually fixate on the "bird": the sounds and images in our immediate world, the people and activities around us, our thoughts and feelings, and all our stories about what we think is happening. During most moments of our day, the bird we are fixated on is our own self-narrative. We are living in a movie with one featured star who is often a deficient, dissatisfied, anxious self. Imprisoned in beliefs and feelings about this limited self, we overlook the vast world beyond that movie, the awake and tender awareness that holds our experience.

The more we become mindful of passing thoughts, emotions, and sensations, the more we find ourselves abiding in the sky of awareness itself. This gives rise to a liberating insight: I am not my thoughts. I don't have to believe my thoughts.

Our incessant self-stories cannot begin to reflect the mystery, beauty, and limitless creativity of who we are. Becoming mindful of thinking and remembering the vast sky of awareness that our stories move through is the pathway to homecoming and freedom.

🌿 REFLECTION For a few minutes turn your attention to your thinking process. Notice how thoughts suddenly arise and then slip away. Where do they come from? Where do they go? What is aware of thinking right now? Turn your attention gently to the awareness that is aware. Relax back into that wakeful openness. Let go and just Be.

*There is a mysterious, fluid, and intrinsically
awake and tender awareness beyond the virtual reality
of thinking. Choose to open to that larger reality.
By realizing you don't have to believe your thoughts,
you can open to freedom.*

SEEING BEHIND THE MASK

There's a joke I like to tell my classes when we're looking at the question of identity: A man arrives at work one morning, late for an office meeting. "Where've you been?" his boss asks. The man answers, "I just saw a clown outside in front of the building." One of his colleagues asks: "Well, was it a real clown, or just a person dressed up as a clown?"

When I share this in a class, there's usually a brief pause—I can hear the wheels turning—and then laughter. We all get it. There's the mask and there's the person behind the mask, and sometimes they get conflated.

The word "person" is derived from the ancient Greek term *persona*, which referred to the masks actors wore to represent certain humans, animals, or gods. In our daily lives, we habitually put on our own personas to suit particular situations. But unlike the actors and audience in ancient Greece who knew these were masks to be removed after the performance, we often get identified with our personas. We might routinely present the knowledgeable, capable mask or the anxious, insecure mask. A coworker might be wearing the judgmental, angry mask. Our core personas are made up of our deepest fears and earliest defenses, and rather than knowing how to put them aside, we often come to believe they are who we really are.

If we move through life trapped behind these masks, we miss out on connection and intimacy with our world. In relating to ourselves and others, we forget the awareness and love that animates our true being.

The blessing of remembering comes with mindful awareness as we witness the changing thoughts, feelings, and emotions that live through us. In the stillness and clarity of presence, we see our masks for what they are: temporary (and sometimes useful) personas but not our essential Being. And with presence we see past the masks of others to the consciousness looking out through their eyes, the tenderness residing in their hearts.

REFLECTION Bring to mind a mask or persona
you most consistently assume. Notice the
thoughts and feelings associated with that
mask. Now bring yourself back to this very
moment and notice the changing flow of

your experience right now: sounds, thoughts, feelings, sensations. Ask yourself: *Who or what is aware of all that is happening?* Let yourself dwell in this presence, the openhearted awareness beyond any persona you might put on. What would your life be like if you could hold your personas lightly, remembering that they are not who you really are? How might this change the way you relate to others?

"I'M AN UNDO"

One of the great myths about meditation is that we do it to gain something: more insight, more blissful experiences, more joy, more compassion. While all those benefits might arise through meditation, they come from letting go, letting be—not grasping onto anything.

Swami Satchidananda, a spiritual teacher from India who played a major role in introducing yoga practices to the West, was once asked by one of his students if it was necessary to become a Hindu like him in order to practice yoga. The Swami smilingly answered: "I am not a Hindu, I'm an Undo."

As Hinduism and all great faiths teach, spiritual awakening is a process of undoing our habitual reactions, letting go of believing in our thoughts and identifying with our emotions. Like a snake shedding its skin, we shed the limiting identities that we've outgrown. By Undoing, we allow the natural intelligence and love that is our true nature to flow freely through us.

IS THIS UNIVERSE A
FRIENDLY PLACE?

When my mother was in her eighties, she moved in with us and began accompanying me to my Wednesday night meditation classes. After a few weeks she assigned herself the job of welcoming anyone who looked lonely, uncomfortable, or as if they felt they didn't belong. The other job she assigned herself was commenting on my talk during our ride home after class. A philosophy major from Barnard, she took great pleasure in our discussions, and even if she agreed with the overall sentiment of a talk, she wouldn't hesitate to take issue when something I'd said seemed to require a leap of faith.

One night I had given a talk on our basic goodness. I shared some well-known words, often attributed to Albert Einstein: "I think the most important question facing humanity is 'Is the universe a friendly place?' This is the first and most basic question all people must answer for themselves."

My understanding is that there's a fundamental benevolence in our universe, and trusting this gives rise to activity that serves our collective understanding, peace, and well-being. In my talk, I had explored ways that meditation awakens our capacity for presence, compassion, and love, explaining that while this basic goodness may be covered over, trusting that it's our innate potential draws it forward and frees our heart.

Well, this provided great fodder for our talk on the drive home! My mother's fine philosophical mind engaged full throttle. "Where's the basic goodness in racism, social injustice, capital punishment, humans violating each other, and destroying the Earth?" she asked. "Where is the Universe's goodness during tornadoes or droughts? And what made goodness more basic than badness or evil? I'm voting for neutral at best," she concluded, satisfied with having made her point.

My mother certainly was voicing what many wonder about. Clearly, there's no way to argue or prove that love and awareness is more primary than aggression, violence, and fear. In fact, in our own lives few of us have avoided aggression, and none of us is immune to fear. In terms of basic goodness, we know that self-doubt and feelings of being flawed at the core are not uncommon. And certainly when we see others who cause great suffering, it's hard to detect their basic goodness.

And yet . . . we long to trust we have intrinsic value, beautiful qualities, and capacities that are beyond our reactive emotions, obsessive thoughts, and imperfect behaviors. We long to feel connection with others, beyond the inevitable conflicts. We long to belong to a timeless loving presence that can carry us through this living dying world. And embedded in and giving rise to our longing is the deep sense that what we long for is possible. In quiet moments of genuine presence and caring, do we not feel a homecoming, an experience that we are part of something whole and connected?

All people must answer for themselves that basic question about fundamental benevolence. And our answer arises out of our own deepest experience. Although I couldn't offer my mother logical proof that we live in a friendly universe, I did share with her something that has been a guiding light for me: the intention to live *as if* loving awareness is our deepest essence.

For all my mom's conceptual sparring, during her final years she was increasingly living in that spirit of trust and finding a deep measure of peace. She would become still with wonder at a tree silhouetted against a darkening sky. She remained always interested in others, and her appreciative listening, kindness, and acceptance brought out their best. Perhaps the most repeated testimony at her memorial was that people felt their own goodness and value in her presence. She might argue from her grave about *basic* goodness, but she lived with a love for the goodness in all people, dogs, and other creatures she encountered.

Recognizing and trusting basic goodness as intrinsic to our own true nature does not arise through thinking. Rather, as we step out of our thoughts (again and again) and bring a gentle, kind, and clear presence to life here and now, we experience that essence for ourselves.

❧ REFLECTION In moments of genuine presence and caring, pause and sense who you are. Can you experience your belonging to a vast, wakeful openheartedness? Does this feel like a homecoming? Can you feel that same capacity for love shining through the eyes of humans, dogs, and other beings?

A PRAYER FOR MIA

I was in the room when my granddaughter Mia was born, and my heart broke open with the blessing of this ordinary and profound miracle of witnessing a new Being come into life. She was beautiful and whole, and to be there as she first opened her eyes in awareness of this world was deeply moving. A prayer for her arose inside me—may she trust her goodness. May she trust the awareness, intelligence, and love that are the truth of who she is.

As I have watched Mia grow and develop, I continue to hold this prayer for her—that no matter what challenges she meets in life, may she always remember her own goodness and that of all beings. In this way she will know true happiness and help awaken awareness and love in the hearts of others.

Especially in times of increased fear and dividedness, our world needs this new generation to cherish the life within and around them. How else will there be healing for our world?

HAPPY FOR NO REASON

I've learned a lot about happiness from my almost daily walks on the hilly trails by the Potomac River. I once had very clear criteria for what made the best walk: favorite time of year (early spring, budding greens), preferred weather (sunny, mild), best times to walk (sunrise, sunset), number of humans around (none).

Of particular value was seeing something unusual, say a beaver or tundra swan. And bottom line, walks were the very best when I was feeling light, agile, and pain free. Oh, how my mood would soar, grateful and happy, when all the boxes were checked. But I started noticing how easily complaints could slide in when some of my ideal parameters weren't met—when they were undercut by cold drizzly days or Sunday crowds or cranky knees.

Out for a walk one evening, I finally got it. As I celebrated the glorious full moon coming up on the horizon, I realized the obvious: happiness that depended on fulfilling my ideal walking preferences was like only being satisfied when the moon was full!

In Buddhist teachings, there are two kinds of happiness. One arises when life is the way we want it—beautiful weather, loving and harmonious relationships, accomplishment at work, our bodies feeling good. This kind of happiness is dependent on Things Going Our Way. The other kind—Happy for No Reason—doesn't depend on what is happening in our life, but rather is the freedom of our heart when we are unconditionally present, resting in an awake, open awareness. No matter what is going on, we basically sense that all is well.

After the full moon realization, Happy for No Reason began creeping into my walks. I'd find myself appreciating natural beauty even on cold, gray days, enjoying the sense of fellowship when the trails were crowded, regarding my hurting joints with tender care not discouragement. One day I set out for my walk with a stomachache and some anxiety about my to-do list (not ideal). I made my way up a steep, icy trail (not preferred), and when I reached the top, I saw that someone had dropped a wrapper on the ground (litter, bad). As I paused to look around, I took stock of how I was actually feeling, despite the unpleasantness.

I was struck by what I noticed. I didn't mind how things were—this was as good a walk as any. And I was feeling happy. Happy for No Reason. When I looked at my experience in that moment, I could see that happiness was arising from simply being present and aware. And with that presence came a sense of belonging to the life within and around me, just as it is. I could notice my physical discomfort and anxiety, I could pick up the litter and still sense a fundamental well-being.

While my daily walks continue to lean toward very pleasant, I have found Happy for No Reason extending to other parts of my experience—the pain when I'm feeling disconnected from others, the anxiety when I'm worried about failing at something, the fear and grief for those who are struggling, my sorrow for our Earth. When these experiences are held in unconditional and tender presence, a basic sense of well-being continues. Having space in our heart for whatever happens, for the moon in all its phases, opens us to the freedom of Happy for No Reason.

REFLECTION Bring to mind a recent time when you've felt happy. Was it only because life was going your way? As you move through your day, pay attention to those moments when a feeling of well-being arises without reason, regardless of circumstances. (It does happen!) Sense how the quality of your own presence gives rise to that well-being.

THE LION'S ROAR

Over the years the Dalai Lama has met with Western Buddhist teachers a number of times, offering guidance and discussing what they encounter in their students. One year, at a conference in Asia, the teachers asked him what he thought was most important to convey to those seeking spiritual inspiration. His immediate response was they should encourage their students "to trust the power of their hearts and awareness to awaken through all circumstances."

In Tibetan teachings, this level of trust is sometimes referred to as the Lion's Roar, expressing the confidence, power, and joy that comes from knowing that we can open to life, that our heart can be present with whatever comes our way.

Let yourself imagine what it would be like to live every day with the Lion's Roar, trusting that whatever arises, including the greatest losses and the deepest fears, has the potential to awaken wisdom and love.

THESE PRECIOUS MOMENTS

One year Zen master Thich Nhat Hanh was scheduled to lead a weekend retreat near my home. My dear friend Luisa Montero-Diaz and I decided to go together. We both were parents as well as being very involved as meditation teachers, so this was a wonderful opportunity to have a break and to share some time together in a special context.

After two days of offering his heart-opening teachings, Thay, as his students call him, ended the weekend by inviting us all to pair up for a concluding practice. Luisa and I, standing side by side, turned to each other and bowed as instructed, acknowledging the Buddha in each other. Then Thay asked us to embrace our partner, not in the quick, friendly way we typically do with friends, but to remain connected, taking three long, deep breaths. "With the first breath," he said, "softly say to yourself, 'I am going to die.'" With the second breath, we were to silently consider our partner: "You are going to die." And with the third breath: "We have just these precious moments together."

Luisa and I had known each other for years, and what a gift it was to realize how precious our time together actually was. As we released our embrace and stood together in silence, I regarded her with great tenderness, seeing her unique and wondrous beauty. And through her smile and shining eyes I could sense her feeling the same for me. This openhearted presence carried us as we left the retreat and journeyed back home to our busy lives. And what we now also carried was that poignant remembrance we had shared with each other—that everything we value will pass away, that we have here and now "just these precious moments together."

STANDING STILL

I was in college when I first started attending yoga classes. I lived near enough so that after class I could walk home along a tree-lined pathway, which was always enjoyable. One particular evening in early spring was so beautiful that I felt inspired to continue walking for a while. I remember the fragrance of the fruit trees blossoming, the feeling of the gentle breeze on my skin, and the quietness in my mind. At a certain point, I found myself standing perfectly still, realizing that my body and my mind were in the same place at the same time. I wasn't rushing ahead with my thoughts; I wasn't mulling over the past. There was a simple sense of presence, and everything was sacred, mysterious, and entirely alive.

Our bodies live in the present moment, but our minds time travel. When body and mind are in the same place at the same time, we discover the creative presence that animates our Being.

OUR TRUE HOME

The space within our bodies and the space that fills this universe is one continuous space, filled with the light of awareness. No inside, no outside. No self, no other. This boundless, undivided space of awareness, with its infinite expressions of aliveness, is our true home.

A HEART READY FOR ANYTHING

Freedom arises from a heart that is ready for anything. This teaching from a Burmese meditation master guides us in living with courageous presence. Our habitual assumption is that we're not prepared enough, that we can't handle what's around the corner. What if instead of tensing against the future, you assume that your heart is ready and available for however this uncontrollable life unfolds? Perhaps you can sense how this might free you to live fully the life that is before you, right here and now.

When our hearts are ready for anything, we are free to love without holding back, free to reach out when others are hurting, and free to celebrate the beauty and mystery of our world. We are free to live from the creative and boundless awareness that is our true nature.

THE FRAGRANCE OF AWARENESS

On the spiritual path, one of our greatest illusions is that we are *on our way* to being wiser and more loving—and that this will only happen sometime in the future after we have done the right practices, after we have found the right teacher, after we read the right books. In truth, the loving awareness we long for is not outside ourselves, not down the road and somewhere else. It is the essence of who we already are.

A beautiful story from ancient India captures this understanding. One day a little musk deer noticed a beautiful and irresistible fragrance in the air. Deeply entranced by its beauty, he set out to find where it was coming from. He searched relentlessly, day and night, until at last, exhausted by his search, he fell to the ground and gave up. As he curled into himself, his horn pierced a tiny sack on his belly and the air filled with the precious scent he had been wildly searching for. At that moment the musk deer realized that what he was pursuing had been emanating from his own being all along.

No matter how far we may wander, no matter how intensely we search, the awakened tender awareness we are seeking is already within us, a half-breath of remembrance away. This essence of our Being can be realized at any time when we arrive in the stillness of full presence.

We sense the depth of our being in the night sky,
in the mystery of silence, of stillness.
In these moments of objectless awareness,
there's a wordless homecoming,
a realization of pure being.

TRUTH OR LOVE?

During my early years of spiritual practice, I sometimes found myself wondering which was deeper:
my longing to know Truth or my longing to experience Love. Which one was guiding and energizing
my path the most? Deep down I knew that it
wasn't an either/or, but still I'd swing between an
intense yearning to dissolve into boundless loving
presence and an equally compelling urge to know
Truth, the nature of Reality.

At times I'd open to a luminous field of loving
awareness and realize there was nothing beyond—
the entire creation was part of my heart. In those
moments of intimacy with all life, *This was It*,
the sacred purpose of the path. At other times,
in utter stillness and openness, there would be a
clear recognition of the empty, transient nature of
self and of all existence. Those moments of simply
Being nourished insights, wisdom, and a profound
cherishing of Truth.

Over the years it became increasingly clear that
Truth and Love are intertwined. Like facets of a
single jewel, they are aspects of one reality—Truth
reflected through the mind and Love through the

heart. Together they express the freedom of our awakening spirit.

As the Indian sage Sri Nisargadatta Maharaj so beautifully teaches: "Love says 'I am everything.' Wisdom says 'I am nothing.' Between these two my life flows."

ACKNOWLEDGMENTS

Trusting the Gold was nourished by the generosity, goodwill, and care of so many:

The seed was planted by dedicated listeners to my podcast who asked if some of their favorite stories and quotes could be made into a book.

The first movement in that direction came from several of my beloved staff members—Janet Merrick, Barbara Newell, and Christy Sharshel—who gathered and reviewed potential material from my books, talks, and articles.

My acting agent and friend Paul Mahon guided me with his great clarity, skill, and sense of fun, as the book found its home at Sounds True.

Jaime Schwalb, my bright, talented editor from Sounds True, shaped the book significantly when she encouraged me to focus on my own personal stories of discovery. Thanks to Jaime's truly collaborative spirit in envisioning and designing *Trusting the Gold*, the challenges of creating a book for publication became a joyful ride.

My dear friend and editor Shoshana Alexander poured through every story I penned, enhancing them with her creative, literary magic and accompanying me throughout with her enthusiasm, encouragement, love, and humor.

My sister, Darshan Brach, offered her wise heart and sharp eye in multiple reviews all along the way. She and our sister-friend and artist Susan Greene advised on all aesthetics of the book.

The extraordinary talent of artist and illustrator Vicky Alvarez shines bright throughout the book, enlivening these pages with beauty and grace.

And within and among it all, my beloved husband and pup; family and friends; students and colleagues; home-team staff; Insight Meditation Community of Washington (IMCW) friends; Mindfulness Meditation Teacher Certification Program (MMTCP) staff, mentors, and participants; richly diverse teachers from all ages; my nonhuman friends; and this precious Earth, our home, all continue to nurture my trust in the gold. A most grateful loving bow to the goodness flowing through each of you.

NOTES

Speaking and Receiving Difficult Truths

"I want to unfold . . ." These lines by Rainer Maria Rilke appear in a poem ("I am much too alone in this world") in *Rilke's Book of Hours: Love Poems to God* translated by Anita Barrows and Joanna Macy (NY: Riverhead Books, 1997).

"An honorable human relationship . . ." Adrienne Rich, *On Lies, Secrets, and Silence: Selected Prose 1966–1978* (NY: W. W. Norton & Company, 1979).

Every Day, No Matter What

"I missed . . . 'making regular visits' to myself . . ." This refers to a line in the poem "A Mouse and a Frog" by Jelaluddin Rumi in *The Essential Rumi*, translated by Coleman Barks with John Moyne, A. J. Arberry, and Reynold Nicholson (NY: Castle Books, 1997), 80.

The Boundary of Our Freedom

"That hurt we embrace becomes joy . . ." From the poem "Silkworms" by Jelaluddin Rumi in *The Glance: Songs of Soul-Meeting*, translated by Coleman Barks (NY: Penguin Compass, 1999), 66.

Please, May I Be Kind

"A psychological study done at Princeton . . ." John M. Darley and C. Daniel Batson, "From Jerusalem to Jericho: A Study of Situational and Dispositional Variables in Helping Behavior," *Journal of Personality and Social Psychology* 27, no. 1 (1973): 100–108. doi.org/10.1037/h0034449.

Our Secret Beauty

"I suddenly saw the secret beauty of their hearts . . ." Thomas Merton, *Conjectures of a Guilty Bystander* (NY: Doubleday Religion, 1965).

The Bridge Between Longing and Belonging

"Prayer is a bridge between longing and belonging . . ." John O'Donohue from *Eternal Echoes: Celtic Reflections on Our Yearning to Belong* (NY: Cliff Street Books, 1999).

Keeping Company with Grief

"Like the Mother of the World . . ." Pir Vilayat Inayat Khan, *Introducing Spirituality into Counseling and Therapy* (NY: Omega Publications, 1982).

Our World's Fear

". . . the RAIN meditation can bring you back . . ." To learn more about the RAIN meditation, see my book *Radical Compassion: Learning to Love Yourself and*

Your World with the Practice of RAIN (NY: Viking, 2019). For online RAIN resources, please visit tarabrach. com/RAIN.

Remembering the Way Home

"What comes into being gets lost . . ." This quotation, reputed to bĕ from Rumi, was published in Andrew Holocek's *Dream Yoga: Illuminating Your Life Through Lucid Dreaming and the Tibetan Yogas of Sleep* (Boulder, CO: Sounds True, 2016).

Is This Universe a Friendly Place?

"I think the most important question facing humanity is . . ." Though this quote is widely attributed to Albert Einstein, especially on the internet, I couldn't verify it. Still, "Is the universe a friendly place" is a fascinating question, no matter who said it or wrote it.

Truth or Love?

"Love says 'I am everything . . .'" This teaching by Nisargadatta Maharaj is remembered by Jack Kornfield, who studied with the Indian guru, in his book *The Wise Heart: A Guide to the Universal Teachings of Buddhist Psychology* (NY: Bantam, 2009), 68. You can also read the excerpt at jackkornfield.com/identification/.

ABOUT THE AUTHOR

TARA BRACH, PHD, is an internationally known meditation teacher and bestselling author of *Radical Acceptance*, *True Refuge*, and *Radical Compassion*. Each month more than three million people tune in to her podcast, which addresses the value of meditation in relieving emotional suffering and serving spiritual awakening and societal transformation. Tara worked as a clinical psychologist for more than twenty years and currently leads accredited workshops for mental-health professionals. She and her colleague Jack Kornfield offer a Mindfulness Meditation Teacher Certification Program that serves participants from more than fifty countries around the world. As founder and a senior teacher of the Insight Community of Washington, DC, Tara offers meditation retreats and a live-streamed weekly class. Dedicated to the awakening of compassion in our society, she has taught workshops for members and staff of the United States Congress and for judges of the D.C. Superior Court. She brings teachings of mindfulness-based compassion to issues of racism and social justice, environmental justice and sustainability, and animal rights. For more information, visit tarabrach.com.

ABOUT THE ILLUSTRATOR

VICKY ALVAREZ is a visual artist and illustrator with a love for the intimate and contemplative experience of art-making and its ability to reveal and heal. She is inspired by her own inner landscape, glimpses of innocence and simplicity, our human vulnerability, and the mystical. Vicky currently lives between her home countries of England and Spain. She also loves to explore her creativity and emotional realm through dance, nature, and clay. For more information, please visit vickyalvarez.com.

ABOUT SOUNDS TRUE

SOUNDS TRUE is a multimedia publisher whose mission is to inspire and support personal transformation and spiritual awakening. Founded in 1985 and located in Boulder, Colorado, we work with many of the leading spiritual teachers, thinkers, healers, and visionary artists of our time. We strive with every title to preserve the essential "living wisdom" of the author or artist. It is our goal to create products that not only provide information to a reader or listener but also embody the quality of a wisdom transmission.

For those seeking genuine transformation, Sounds True is your trusted partner. At SoundsTrue.com you will find a wealth of free resources to support your journey, including exclusive weekly audio interviews, free downloads, interactive learning tools, and other special savings on all our titles.

To learn more, please visit SoundsTrue.com/freegifts or call us toll free at 800.333.9185.